BE
LABOUR
READING

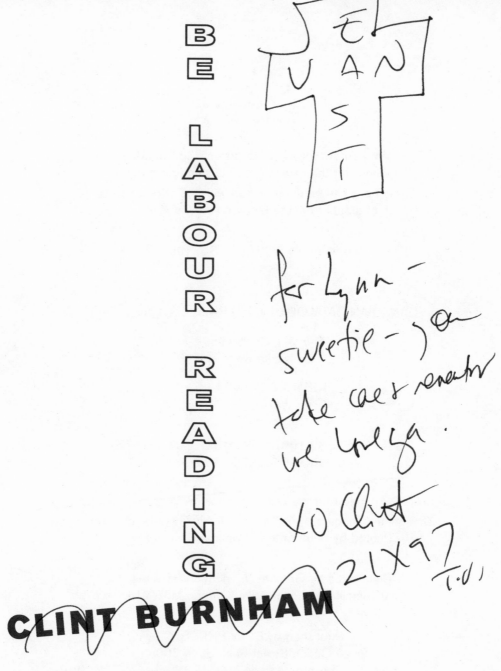

BE LABOUR READING

CLINT BURNHAM

ECW PRESS

for Lynn —
sweetie — *so*
take care & remember
we love ya.

XO Clint
21 X 97
T.O.

THE CANADA COUNCIL | LE CONSEIL DES ARTS
FOR THE ARTS | DU CANADA
SINCE 1957 | DEPUIS 1957

We acknowledge the support of the Canada
Council for the Arts in our publishing program.
This book has been published with the assistance
of grants from the Ontario Arts Council.

CANADIAN CATALOGUING IN PUBLICATION DATA

Burham, Clint, 1962-
Be labour reading

ISBN 1-55022-344-5

I. Title.

PS8553.U665B2 1997   C811'.54   C97-931677-4
PR9199.3.B87E2 1997

Editor for the press: Michael Holmes
Design and imaging by ECW Type & Art, Oakville, Ontario.
Printed by Printcrafters, Winnipeg, Manitoba.

Distributed by General Distribution Services,
30 Lesmill Road, Don Mills, Ontario M3B 2T6.

Published by ECW PRESS,
2120 Queen Street East, Suite 200,
Toronto, Ontario M4E 1E2.

http://www.ecw.ca/press

GORDE HUNTER

and I've always
admired the way
he wrote he
could speak

to the people, had
a common touch with
ellipses, the drawing

man, the drawings
they'd be full of
the most cherry

Gorde! Look out! it's NATO!
oh, it's ok
they're just,
they're just bombing somewhere
now, they're not irrelevant

remember the cold war?
squeaking tape decks?
cheery civilization bhangra
quadraphonic stereo? Harvard Yard?
sure you do
yeah, it's alright now

signature tunes, that's what's ailing you
metric measurement
french canadians
the Partition – those wacky kids – John Belushi, eh?

why didn't 6, here,
that's what I want to know
his picture on the tv garden

unpronounced

beard burn on my inner thigh.
think about it for a moment!
hunter! you were on welfare!
you *know* what it's like

(two puppies)
an ejaculation
pro-choice
imagine that (vs)
the about aids (chorus)
missing someone (us)
brutally cut down in the prime of life,
mixed up

pro-choice — now it seems —
well, don't want to go into it here...

bold face is useful
blackface is out-of-date

italics — well — they've *had* their day.

b.u.m equipment, coke, 3-in-1 oil

cancer of the mouth
pancreitis
three born premature
scar tissue
hobbled legs
free medical
dental plan
serial killer, pension, it's a wonderful life (chile, nicaraugua)

cancer causes cancer
(horoscopes: another poem

fifteen inches of snow in april
september's child

nobody's complaining about grey books
with red lettering — even though *he's* a nazi

it's just mindless entertainment, said the (a)esthete.

you crack me up — you really do, you
know that?

he died one year, I'm not sure when
we read about it in the papers
his hands weren't any good anymore
my dad mentioned it to me

(just now, I stopped writing

SCOTLAND

thin bands of colour in front of me
sometimes it's necessary

not to understand, can't
see that, don't want to
confirming the

theory in the first place
your abbreviations

and mis-quoted signs as
a friend is in the newspaper

and there are pizza joints unhallowed
but not unnoted.

a contrary kitten, and sometimes punishing
yourself with the expectations

of phleg-
matic book colonels and

tufted ears: the early
british generals, a carried

huzza, staples crushed against
indignant

gyproc, but that's
no surprise: I ran into him

and discussed weight gain
thumping around us and

sometimes you're right about
the shoes, but it's important not

to let them get in the
way of a good conversation

there are many experts
with old boy ties around

their waists, seducing men
like you change mechanics,

but that doesn't mean the
images are everywhere

or equally free I've
been accused enough to

think I am one, and like
you can go on about it if

there's an end, sometimes
skies fall out of the book

and sometimes the other
way around I read an article

about them at work the other
day, these incredible

pressures, surveillance
cameras in my neighbourhood

and video flourishes as artform
and on tv. the

central theme
parked isn't

appropriate clothing
ideas with words

I can't believe I used
that many to

get here
books are too lux-

urious to justify
lined hands and we

do anyway

II   .

sometimes offices seem
like lined buildings,

the hallow core of
belief steadily chipped

rock in a school-
yard. and an intense

loneliness rains
four broken contracts

in the shrieking cold
an airplane on a field

of white paper you can circle
around and see the loading

dock, confirm reports I
don't think you got gut

twine two loose mine, Can-
adian boys over there

need our support
in case you forgot

and the letters 'fe'
float, entire

pages of harrassed
titles

a grilling for the
cheeseburger, now

relegated to an image-
repertoire

and child-abuse
for me torn

the shit: hash pipe after
a poetry reading

or just before I
introduce you fucking

english: probably and
a lima head, cigarette

stubble, breasts, a little
dog's head & suddenly

a gun, man's legs, far
away, a car, high on the

suspension

III

& labour banners its waves —
a cheap start, lines

you can't ignore, invented
parentheses, and real

parents, feeling as if
for different

societies, unliberated
and berating, scolded

and sodden, tides
calculating

holy cat!, she's
thrown out the truck

magazine after
cutting out her

braver than ever (questions
that answer themselves,

eavestroughing serpentine
in its memory is a sub-

routine of desire, I am
the last moral being, and

I have to kill you
first, but

my grandfather left
his hedgeclippers in

his other pants
somewhere in Burnaby,

B.C.

IV

hospitals grow diseases
and the punks are

petulant, destroyed
by the beer they steal

from ungulate drunks, lining
up to lift lips to teat

wearing your eyes out
with overpriced flowers

delivered to deafening
clubs by thick-fingered

men in cloth caps (lines
just erased accuse

and the quiet white tubes
line drug deals cells,

metaphors failing
before the graffitti

and elevator

RENT-A-MARXIST

Oh heteroclite pessimism!

Menstruating tongues wag

i jerk off the plaster horse over your open mouth
get out the new english translation of the yellow pages
i'd like to dribble the illegal chopshop near the horse farm down your wrists

a debate over labourer versus worker
dicks dump dumbly all over the place

the oldest working stiffs
a tradition of metric historiography
my saliva'll dissolve the encrusted fluid
on the khakis with a hole in the crotch i got for 2 bucks at value village

no please mark laba wears khakis
i'd rather castrate myself immortal
hit the immutable scission
if you'd let me strangle you

you like the way her arms are held back
around an olympian tower?
what are you a girl?

the rants that malcolm rodney gave us
will do in a pinch
a punch a penile colony
but don't rip me too much
i want to ride my bike later and see a movie

the will to power runs a few degrees above most folks ...
ah my hairy tit i do love looking down at you

AS HER (AIR TRAFFIC)

I don't know, what do you think
of someone climbing up
a mountain, his dad
in a jar in his hands? The day
was windy,
and his daughter was with him
(she was going through a divorce,
times were tough all over). Unfortunately,
living on the planet for fifty-
eight years and always having a steady job
never prepared him for the greasy ashes.
So much for the educational power of tv.

Of course,
he could have refused
the request, stayed home
watched the Bills
clobber the Packers.
Once, years earlier,
he'd been a
scab at a bakery
came home with his face bleeding
a tooth hanging on
by a thread. His
father, who never
bought life insurance or
savings bonds, drove him to
the hospital in the cadillac
he threw up in
at his high school graduation.

Then there are
the alternatives – what if *your*
son came home with his face smashed by ugly unionists.
OK you don't have any kids
and you wish you had a union the way you get fucked
over at work.
But what if.
The point is, the ashes
remained, hung around like
a damp shower curtain, and
who wants to touch *that*. It
was like he was saying, hold
on, I'm not really gone, you can't
get rid of me that easily.

What happened was the daughter got back with her husband.
They made some adjustments, got
some counselling, and now she's pregnant. It's
going to be a boy, and it'll
have the same name as her grandfather. But like she
told her dad, the baby
isn't being named *after* the grandfather,
it'll just have the same name.

MOST NON-LAWYER CANADIAN CITIZENS ON THE CBC

Oh dart sin souk, soothes often
Dave errs 10 leave it bin gold naw site
Does auger seat den Himalaya offed them
Ash felt dreamt inherit in Zelig kite
Oh does he effect grinding bleed bub!
Deal show & his height drugging Leigh bah.

HOUSE ORGAN

he's up in heaven
with his old lady
throwing one-liners @ St. Peter
i've been in meetings
with permanent members
of the Japanese mining community
and i want to maintain
their interest in the fusion
of heroin and heavy water in holes
five miles down = a million km up
or a rugby shirt
and buying the sheer joy
of rolling in the mud with
his cigars and martinis
and his fondness for
the company of pretty
young women
he made
old age
out to be an extension
of the prime of life
not a
back bedroom
motherfucken modernist
made it seem for a while
as if he had no
intention of leaving at all
but what does that
sudden splatter inversion
milk suddenly splashing
the wall of the glass

i thought i just put gin
"wave it in the direction of Paris"
ice shaken
how come it's creamy
later a stir
fry up hard bread
maundering around
the globe, finding
the best deals
a steal
a scream if things
are in the way
"marketing, like poetry
is about language"
"about using my talent"
"get out of this bor-
ing well-paid job"
"the wealthy working class"
"trade, like art
recognizes no boundaries"
except those of authentic cultures
it's okay to write
"like this" if you want to
not if you have to
schizophrenia is a
chemical imbalance
a barley sandwich
wrapper
in each hand
that's why he made
fun of me
for walking on my toes

gonna be a ballerina
motherfucker
(my name for dad)
though he didn't
that's the suspicion, any-
way back in the day
O.P. if she
migrates to a thicker sock
greys on trays'll
mower down
as if listening to
lo-fi'll
make them young
again the declaration
of independence
was about handscrawled
cassette covers (maybe
it will who's
to say, follow
the bouncing
balls on him
sing, hang
with the rowdy
man in an
rcmp
uniform, learn
how to
hotwire a car
and native customs
from a 60s tv
— he walked
and took the bus

from the forest down to
hastings and main
to be a jr.
forest ranger
jr. gen'l kit
(don't call it that)
marker on gun tape
– ah, nostalgia!,
that cheap canadian tire
duct tape only good for
hand signals
to raise the boom
but lower the load
and ed sullivan
(shabbas goy in the house)
used wayne and
shuster to keep
people from channel
surfing - back then
you were on your
knees, saliva
on the cookies
keep my place
and adventures
in rainbow country
of float planes
not boat drinks
or
a chic-chi and a prince
albert thru his
cock a hot
rod or pemmican in

my eight
year old mouth
learning the words
prick and mda
in boy scouts
on joey small-
wood's farm
a tea towel and
a newfie joke
to celebrate
25 years of
belonging
submarine
3-dollar bills
a parachute

FROM GIRL TO THE AIR FORCE

a potsmokers pussy and a shaved pout
Harry's full of horse shit has a moustache and everything
a fish & game patch on his jacket still
his still drawing breath and soft black moustache
a conundrum in the drum corps empty to the core
marching and then praying and then driving at the train
acid and jet planes over the base teen centre
pedal near the forest master-corporals and captains
mechanics and doctors and a cross-dressing dj
with an ex in the maritimes and a kid and a falsetto moustache
he was sexy in a dress so was she but better
this time or maybe another time but he looked sexy
a dress and a church and a ruthless division coming
police patrolling black stationwagons
humorous carcinogenic phone calls
cops harrass kids pilots eject upside down stoned and dying
stiletto cold war caverns hangars of narrative bombers
sirens identification cards the woods run round

I'VE TASTED YOUR BLOOD

children play
foreign tongues
I lick
your
furred ceiling

LET'S HAVE A ROD RIOT

hey i don't like your rock melody
annie get your speech there's work to be done
semen is the word — spread it
look at your muscle and make it grow
you think you've got troubles you drive-in dick
my wood butch'd be better than your butcher would
they're converting dirt into dollars oil into revenue
buy a view today at pain and wasting
a cell phone on the bus can give rise to
excuse me I don't bum smokes from the police
they better pick up these butts we live here
I have a hash pipe the size of an inhaler
this bong water's kinda skanky if only this was egypt
you think you've got problems your drive-in cunt isn't my needle-nose dick
and someone'd change it for me don't draw lions on those lines
come on my face — the dog can lick it off later

MAGIC MOUNTAIN

On vacation before I became an engineer, I stayed
at this motel in the Swiss Alps

It had air conditioning
and I stayed inside
watching the war on CNN

I never met any of the guests
and left a week later,
refreshed

GROSS STORY

today when we were at this Indian restaurant today. There
was this family, and this kid, about 7 or 8 who kept sitting on
his dads
lap and kissing him. I'm talking full tongue in mouth, sloppy
wet with
hands around the neck. Total make out. And they would all be
giggling
while we dipped our nan in our lentils, chins on the floor. And
then the
dad would start making out with his wife, giving her the tongue and
stuff,
whispering and biting her ear. And then 3 or 4 minutes later the
kid
would get all excited again and start Frenching daddy. Like, wow:
nothing
better than tasting mom on daddies tonsils!!

PROPS 2 JIM SMITH

sound track tattoo
another nose-ring
I'm really sorry about

I got home, & my brother
(not oregano on welfare)
accused me
where were you &
I said to my dead
I'm your SON
RESPECT ME
act like a man
full of grief
I screamed at the wind:
Rilke? Hölderlin? Pantera?

potential harm resulting
in hyperextension of the
lower back
high gormless
immersion coerce in ganga

you're always there
even if it's a message
machine

embarrassed in a restaurant
at what you said to the waitress
like the marxist scholar
wasn't SM during rem

but he looked like my father
who has the same name as
a guyanese leader
trotskyist economist
harvard political scientist

electoral patterns – chimeras
shibboleth – can't
tell you how to lambent
(front rhyme

she erased you suck
by the yeastie girls
offended the brewery

I'm a cultural at
taché at the banana
republic the stain of the mirror
for paul, have an
encyclopedic mind (un-
fortunately, it's either
the new book of
knowledge or that
means the encyclopedia
americana (and my
bike helmet (soundgarden, et al)
(pace) looks like a mc-
donald's hairnet
over a styrofoam box

air bubble head rap
big hair journalism
puff pieces, rice courier

Cantax's better than Wintax,
for professionals
I hope you'll come back
to me next year
but I prefer Winfax

& Amy Tan's *Enter the Wu-Tang Clan*
Jack Lord is goddess

crispy hair & puffed rice
better or (crunchy hair) first
thing in the morning (or 2 or
3 orgasms — efficiently create
your own life mode —
depending on your sex
or whatever
hilarious

machiavelli, I mean michelangelo
was a ceo of his time, perfected the
use of agent ochre to turn the umbrian
countryside into the stone ages and
make it into a parking lot (better
skateboarding & rollerblading)

angst, father, long-term TV (T)

I want to go into labour
law, but not represent
welfare workers (when I
thought that she was
wrong) — howard petch,
adam west, the others
creative cantina

but my whole thing with
community and social services

and I don't know how
else I'll get in there

I'm more interested in a cushy job?
unless it's grassroots in parkdale.

wearing skirts that's what it
would entail:
nylons even in the summer

can you imagine wearing
(making 80 grand
a suit jacket with a baby
(carrot)
in a frame over
it

they don't let in
people like me (well
they do eventually

and you can't change your experience
you can't win if you don't
have the right experience

all about metacommentary
middle culture red pumps
do

rain net peds end:

I feel like a blowjob

TALKING TO BORIS

hello rick, my mind is a fridge
my mime is afraid I need my paycheque
it's going to rain and my
fridge is outside, on the
sidewalk, covered in
white paint and old
inflated stickers – rick, this
is important, if you can't
see me, at least listen
to me
I kept Christmas trees in
it the last year of my life,
rick – can I tell you rick,
can I call you rick?
would you rather – wellness?
Moscow? Murder? Mafia? Mule? I don't –
I don't know rick, sorry,
Mr. Boris, how can you
appreciate my life here, on the
14th floor of a grain elevator,
the stairs aren't working, it's
a monochromatic prairie day and
I only have colour film –
won't do for a faded fridge, batteries
inside, chock-a-block with xmas needles
sparkling forth of july ...
rick, should I have put
'u' in there? no, not
you, not you Mr. Rick
Boris sir, a u, the
letter u, you know the
letter U don't you, the
second last letter in
paycheque?

listen up chum.
buddy. pal.
you take the highway,
I'll take the byway,
I don't care, honest
harold, I mean, look
at it my way, I've got
a family to support

okay. I was stretching it
there, I'll admit it. I
never had a bridge, and
all day saturday I
keep a pot slowly simmering
on the sheet metal covering
the knobs. so
you know I'm not
serious about the needle
park, you know, umm ...
but my mind is a
fridge nonetheless rick,
it's like I tell you,
like I was saying to
Mister McHugh just
yesterday, & to
the mrs.

and there are memories
I haven't snapped the
plastic lid off
since

CAN THE MUSIC

Face is lying face up there
over two boys playing possum girl

mirrors are easier to
handle then boyfriends arrive, one
at a time, a tape stretched

across the river warns the platoon
of their imminent uniformity,
banyan, hercules, the

balkanization of the balkans,
cancelled stamps and rubbery cod fisheries

condom coffee, old ho's in miami vice episodes
the levantine (graham greene
(actor or writer?) punk through the ages

whenever black guys
kill white people
we want gun control

cold coffee and milk (to
appear your piece of
mind

bra, panties (thong
boxers, unitard, big blunts

lite jazz
canadian winters in florida
political in trieste, the

twisted sister or pantera rosa?

happiness I feel writing
this letter to you is

al-moky (the first
lebanese I ever met: actress, no longer uttered

i think catholics
should abjure factionalism, be more universalist in their outlook, not let
religious differences

emily carr, jack shadbolt, burn old books and teachers
protractor, divider, compass, ruler
roach clip, hash pipe, rolling papers

politically correct sharp pencils to push the filter in
to my small harp

how can you be angry with me
if you can't even spell my name?

(if I knew it, I'd like to be
buried in my wedding dress, although
I'm not married, to

drumkit, bass guitar, flying v
mosh pit, slam dancing, pogo, stage dive

to write
about selling
t-shirts with

that'd crack you up
this is in code so it won't interfere

listen:
paint and cappucino

last summer was the best
winter of my life, and so is
this one (details survey,
I've decided to
let my hair grow (sorry,
it keeps slipping out
of my grasp) true 2–3
years after

how did this logos in the sense
of reason and under-
standing achieve domination
over being in the beginning
of Greek philosophy?

she's sweating in
another room: thanks
to good police work

the election's the day
before I start my job, but
after that,
irridescent – hemp,
blue denim shirts marching and
beating up blacks

ROBOT FELLATION

it seemed as though that was
it for a while, the roads were
clear, the scholarship
asshole! conversationals
induce discussions about
rent in our society, maybe
your hair, the feeling a goose
has in the water
legs
webbed mattresses and military
belts, but
if not for now
(as if it were for heaven

CARS CAN TAKE IT EASY NOW
POLITICIANS
HAVE NO WARES FOR SALE
the alternative
lies are easier to
(various: starlings, I have
to go back and re-read the classics
if you're on the radio one more time,
I'll tie a metal band around your leg

his arms tickle me, but
at least I'm not Laurie
and in the end, you know
that's how it slides
(into disk collection containers
grandrather clauses
televisual impacts of bald coitus

a czech word, I asked my firehose the
wool rations: you'll have to give up your doctor
think about it for a minute

I'm back in the groove of things and
regardless of the girdle (bacon, for
heaving along quite well, thank you
it's MY birthday, "I'll get 'drunk' "[3]
but don't you never no mind: we
want to tie to tell a story

corruption's rife in the mafia

sometimes it pays not to be TOO spunky, the main
reason for faltering US dominance in the text industry

she was looking forward to
the view out the window
a subway is often in front of people and
doorways, locked, my arm in the rubber
NO GLVE is not allowed as a licence plate
(& licence pltes are not allowed as condoms
so there's no homophobia

sometimes I WISH GAY JUST MEANT SLACK ANTS
but rods change their meaning (if only GAP didn't

BLIND RANCH HANDS

I was just writing a poem about you or to you, it's 8:11 on Sunday night. I was glad to be doing some writing, to be writing a poem, even if I don't know if it'll be any good, because I've been drinking a lot this weekend & smoking pot & hash & I hate being lazy and not having done anything all weekend. We went to a thing at Mike's on Thursday night, a guy from the states talked about a painter, he was pretty good, but later David said, why do those guys always wear khakis and a striped shirt. The New England property owner look, tieless. & we smoked some hash & after the Upper Canada beer gave out we drank white wine from a box. Mistake number one. I spend all day Friday at work recovering from the hangover. But conversation was very quick & sparkling & witty. We talked a lot about Toronto in the early 60s, Gerrard Street then. Good history.

The next day after work I came downtown with Paul & I went & bought some pot & hash, $60 for an eighth of pot & a gram of hash. We went out to hear some loud music at the ElMo & sat next to kids from Hamilton. They were mildly excited that we wrote for Fuck & one of them brought Paul a glass of water. Saturday we didn't do much in the day: smoked some dope. Julie had gone out the night before with a girlfriend. Saturday night we went to a friend's place & drank a lot. Got home pretty tired. Got up early today to do stuff at the magazine & to go to a talk about appropriation. Pretty pomo stuff, there was a guy there who did a movie about Harvey Keitel I want to see. So I had some dinner a little while ago, some beers, some smoke.

AN EVENING AT HOME

reading about bachelor
dinners, newspaper
article on celibacy and
rhymes with habitat and fat

balzac and coffee

blowjobs come later

thinking about doing
the dishes: in one novel,
they say sisterfucker
in another
daughter fucker

wallah, sadhu

kingstoner: granite, broadloom (over
particle (children, wallphone
sideburns, television antenna
hardwired penis size
evolution, date rape, information

bicycles vs motorcycles
goretex vs leather
panniers vs nivea virgins

halcyon senectitude (swimming in ddt
Seneca College, Ontario senate
Kenorah
part of the problem is fishing
(microvans, mountaingoats: plagiarizing lynx

mendicant
do you want
a clean house
or dog où
sexe

neuter, tapioca, oatmeal hat trick
backwards, wisdom
teething ring, cock ring

children
sentimentalism vs
romance

love, lust, legionnaire's disease
jimmy carter, lesion

jews or gays?
that's obvious
we protest
a macedonian chorus
second generation theories of youth

WERK

van as a germanic cross
Laundry basket eyes
can see the basket case
of kokanee in cans for
easier carrying on
a table made of deals
lined up for christmas
vouchers at a sally
ann williams lake
boots at the outdoor store east

on the bush elders
sun-dried laundry
without a bc overdue
bill (location
as steve said the
deology named place
her manic cross
felt and without
stripping forms
or gloves, hands
handily peeling
and fingers
shortening then
up my ass kangaroo
different prices
across town white

wine socialistists
exotic to news
'aper' shimmering
like an illusion
metaphor across
the pond touching

your skin ugh with
out vag club ecstasy
coke in effect oat mod
curled fingers for
the tuxedo frame and picture
fame breathing farts into
the bedroom eye dick
hardly underneath and
the bed furthermore

class as an issue
of a stapled journal
as you can't see
yourself for the fog
posing in the corner of
an autoparts store is good
undergoing ape transplant
through my war chest
as the strike drags on

*

Dear Lee
            It's Wednesay night, just sitting down
after supper. Teresa had a good day at school, the
teacher

cause when we got here in 1948 there was 17,000 people out of work and a
streetcar strike, early saturday morning, the train was late we got in late and
phoned him he had a phone in his truck she maintained it herself and got
400,000 miles on it we saw it up on the shop in the shop and you couldn't
buy a car if there was one

I was driving in from surrey up clark to the roundhouse and fog, it was foggy I
was behind a bus pacific coach and this guy's behind me and I pull into the

parking lot and he gets out of his car and asks me why I stopped and I said I
worked there how am I going to get out of here now I got him out of there
with a flashlight man

I crocheted that on
her blanket
not downtown you know
cause that's lower class take
him around there and
don't let anyone kiss him
or give him anything
to eat

and if she was having a bridge
party he came in the back
way to where I was washing
her and doing her hair he'd
hold her hair there

pissing into her hair
in the toilet rimmed with

an espresso flavoured
with jojoba shampoo/
conditioner flakes
of dandruff and loose
hair moustache cup

just stand there
you know
looking at me

MINISTRY

well
or
not well, why
does everyone — Lynn,
Paul draw
me with these
little things
on my ears — the
question

trucks — no one
can drive them (really
anymore — not like
you drive cattle
or drunk: lights
glowing snowflakes
aureole, ravines in raves
in saskatchewan — but this one was in
montreal, which isn't a white
walled museum, altho it
was, two hits of acid,
listening to orbit,
moby, trance port

sitting in real veal
fattening pens eating
veal sandwiches and mustard,
mayo most computer games
come with a hot key
so your boss
will think you're working
on a spreadsheet

spread your legs, please

we could hear sexual
harassment wafting
gently over the Partition
eager mouths
screwed into manuals
dexterity and dobermans
on everyone, but
the ministry is an
olive bread sandwich
car, flashing as it turns the
corner to a long,
treeless rural concession road
dear minister: where
is the exit to ecstasy

fishing for a complement
to the poultry-coloured
office machines

discuss corel-draw
with complete strangers (nominalist)
at the last temptation
as teenagers lip
rings fester

affiche, putty, puffy: occam's razor

my nipples itch
in this paragraph,
choking and pulling are okay:
come thru nostrils
like writing thru race
and beer bottles up my ass

are not

(mention he's complex
make sure
you mention he's difficult

I once wrote a poem
hungover, in a hotel lobby,
listening to moby and thinking
about susan howe – he's
his great-grandson

gangsta
vanilla bureaucracy and the villains
is batch processing like
making 100 cookies from
a recipe for 10

yeah but without the vanilla:
flavouring rather than
individual flavour listings

i write them down
cause i can't remember them

NB: maturity = responsible boredoms
can you flag that?
My sex is 4H
Margin
drive, draws, daughter, drought, drew to
visualize the big picture here: in a minor
country, the boot vertigo unfathomable
4 pairs, two people, black

yeah, but less effort &
they can't see I'm
nervous/bejewelled

rower wear co-respondant
shoes (I was conceived as my
parents watched submarine
races from burnaby mountain
and I once wrote "once"
beginning with a w

three curly lines
not applicable
matches physique

do a procedures
system down

DEAR DEAD

Knock me up side the head one more time, knock some sense into
me. I won't show the bruises well I did as we discussed your early
marriage & my premature birth. I was secretary for my class but later
I was supposed to get moved up and didn't he won't adjust. So an X
on my back marks the spot for short hair jokes as she writes on my
neck a tattoo 20 years later the crease marks from a lifetime of
setting into the tractor we had a combine with air and an 8 track
after my dad died it was just me and mom to seed the field fallow
the exhausted dried out spent and dust rolling into she ran away
looking for dad. Give me a good clipping.

Dear dad today at school they investigated me vaginally. I demand
that you ~~protect~~ protest this infraction or infringement on your basic
property rights (fringe under a bra, beads) they could investigate to
see if she had a homosexual past and they talk back in the
schoolyard it's nice asphalt with a good chain link fence to get your
tongue stuck on next thing you know they'll be knocking down your
door with the state police looking for guns and drugs. Now a father
can't tickle his daughter. They didn't check the sons no means no.

My girl she's a smart one she read this pamphlet at school and she
came home and said daddy you're not anything like this it says you
wouldn't want to do anything if you smoked pot and now you can do
things the pain isn't there. I raised them well.

GROUNDWORKS STAND TO

Trenton I need a drink. I got frostbite last night got my tongue stuck on my rifle. Shaved dry. My cold helmet. Shot my sergeant. That's a bad thing, someone said. We came in after fighting French-Canadian engineers.

KURT, DIANA BRUNO STEIN "BOB IN BOSNIA"

almost throw up
brown nuggets in my hand
the pot to edge off the heroine
art wants to be good
the beatles in hollywood
starting work
grandparents ask about my record
it can get me a job don't worry
he phoned collect but she raised hell
parents are invoiced they can under
a clear patch
drainage
mustard jars under my bed
writing poems in barracks
& performing as a spaz
she collected phoney fabric
before the ice cream after pms
knew louis riel
married the daughter
of the regimental
sergeant major

I can feel the bitter
acid still in my mouth,
an inventory of jeans
and sweatshirts a body
found in track pants
disregarded marriages and
secretly writing he
leaves the house with
her trapped in a narrative
where he can only leave
not do anything trapped
like frank sinatra in

a narrative where
he trapped a victim
like frank sinatra
was a victim (keep
on fucking
whining

the gold of my
stomach is mythical,
motherfucker no literally no handcuffs to keep me out of there ancestors and
answers a sudden interest in "rolling a
punk rock stories as if

BAD DATE

Heroin alert there is a new extremely strong heroin now out on the street we have had a number of overdoses reported be extremely careful check it out only use a bit until you are sure of what you are taking fix with someone else and go slowly take care of yourself

Long time bad date caucasian male 5'8" – 5'10" 160–180 lbs blue
or green eyes wavy strawberry blonde hair slightly past shoulder
length freckles glasses sometimes has a moustache facial features
described as "similar to a frog" usually picks up around
quebec/1st/2nd/3rd goes to wherever he can get women cornered
agrees to $100 but doesn't pay used to drive a rambler now drives
a white geo storm his line is that a woman didn't show on time and
she's too late tells woman he saw her and she looks good to him
when he gets the woman alone, he rapes her vaginally, anally and
orally

Caucasian male 6'1" 180 lbs blue eyes blond short feathered hair clean shaven good looking driving older blue 2-door malibu picked up woman at princess & cordova went to ray cam parking lot pay woman $40 for bj after she got him off he demanded $$ back he took her purse and drove away

Pakistani male 5'7" 150–170 lbs has beard 34 years old driving brownish van maybe a mazda picked up woman in waldorf parking lot went to renfrew & 1st agreed to $35 for bj – paid $25 when woman started bj he asked for a feel he began forcing hand inside guy was very brutal

Caucasian male 5'8" 160–170 lbs brown eyes short brown hair walking picked woman up by american hotel went to the viaduct paid $50 for half & half after woman finished date guy grabbed her and started to beat her saying she robbed him

Heavy set male 5'6" brown/black hair short on top long in back
driving black sports car picked up woman at salisbury & pandora
went to fraser arms guy offered to pay a lot of money plus said he
had an 8-ball physically violent and talked dirty when he got woman
to the fraser arms he let her out of the car and drove away leaving
her there

Caucasian male 5'8" 130 lbs brown eyes long brown hair with over grown moustache driving 2-door black monte carlo 79 picked woman up on franklin track agreed to $100 after date guy paid her then when she got out of the car he ran after her she fell down and he punched her when she tried to get up again

Caucasian male 6'2"– 6'3" 225–240 lbs short blond tight wavy hair says his name is steve kicked woman's feet out from under her she started fighting back he then pinned her and dragged her she finally talked her way into getting away

Repeat east indian male 6ft 280 lbs guy does coke tells woman he'll get them high he gets woman to score then rips her off this guy is an asshole and potentially violent

Buying sex from kids is child abuse if you see someone cruising for kids or picking up a kid for a date you can help by reporting their description particularly their licence plate number all reports will be anonymous no one will source you and no one will ask for your testimony call the safety office tell the van drivers let's protect our kids!

ANDERSON

What, was it a Thomas Mann novel, the one where this guy's taking
a train to the mountains to go on vacation? Like it's his girlfriend's
cottage, up in the Muskokas, and he's about to become an engineer,
and he's feeling kind of depressed. So he gets there and he's either
looking at a television report of the G7 meeting in Venice, they show
scuba divers and various — or he's looking at the lake, a tree
hanging its head over the water like it's washing his hair, it's like
he's a real regionalist but still doesn't like reference works too
much, I mean, who wants to carry around the new book of
knowledge, which is how she writes. It's her greatest hit, about the
dairy queen in Victoria, she didn't believe in lesbians and so they
made her into an icon.

A little while ago I read Victor Coleman's attack on Coach House.
He was on the phone but he felt a bit sick. We decided we'd try to
get together later on in the week. He asked me if I'd read the Sun
that day. He had a bible on the table, and some papers in one of
those bags they give you at photocopy shops. But sometimes your
friends are like the characters in bad novels: you wonder how they
could know that much, if it isn't a case of giving away what they
couldn't possibly know. They don't go far enough, you know what I
mean? He's going to think it's an attack, but really it isn't. That's
what she's always paranoid about: not enough boxes, the way
Simon keeps turning up at things. There she was on the street and
he pulled up. I can see I'm just worried about how I use it. The joke
turns on the homolinguistic similarity between "pussy" and "posse,"
but I won't. There was this diorama, of a fetus becoming a baby, a
toddler, a young boy, a teenager, a young man, slightly older, getting
fatter, hunched over, bearded, scraggly, collapsing on a stick,
skeleton and becoming the earth. It was very moving. I ate three
bananas. The robot soared above us, in the sky: it was like we were
in Victoria, or Jonathan Swift.

You don't have to worry about it being a witch-hunt, tho. He just has that one Deep Purple tape, a Nirvana cd, and maybe something else. He was like a model, and I was like a cybertron. It was a video game and a movie: the way he shilled for intellivision. We tried to avoid him but he showed up on the subway platform. We appeared pleased. She was watching me buy a chocolate bar. The Indian families were out in full force, grandmothers, their midriffs exposed, they used to be real party girls in the fifties, and now they're just like hanging out with the family. Once she went to Calcutta and got some new fabric. Her father was furious with her. Now, the hippies like twenty-five years after the fact: historical hippies, from Woodstock to stocks. He ate some watermelon on the ferry ride home (imagine being that prepared) with a plastic fork, out of a freezer container, beige, slipping the seeds out of his mouth.

He saw her in the park, she was flirting with someone who looked like he would when he was older, if you get the idea of the krishna diorama. Reincarnation is oedipal. Then his father found out, and was furious, she had left for another man. They took me around everywhere, I was playing at work with her and she was trying to make track suits (so you can see this was Tehran, not the middle ages) but the boss had a video camera in the workshop and watched from the other room. I wanted a pair of rubber boots. I saw it over a year or almost a year ago. We want them. On the beach, he seemed nicer. He got sand in his shorts. There's a good scene there, and we're getting a lot of support. She changed Japanese to TV.

When she smiled quickly a mole popped up from the neckline of her blouse. Named Rachel ... but that isn't my point. My point is. He took a cigarette from his pack of Camels and lit it. His fingers were long. He leaned back on the couch, flicked his shirt open. If she were a customer and the quiet man with the wide, black hair should come from the back and serve her. She put the bottle into the bag, and crossed the street. A man knelt before her. Do not say struggling, not struggling. She felt the weight of the plastic bag and looked at the shape the Evian bottle made, pulling the bag down with white stretch marks. Small crumbs and other dirt moved into the centre of the glass, pushed by the cloth.

Did you see the poster down there? She walked up to them. She was carrying a white plate with bits of food scattered around the edge. After this, others talking of much the same thing. Overlapping so that everyone. So the thing is, he suicided in fifty-six. Summer, like this. He leaves a note. He corrected his grammar, a verb agreement problem or something. I don't remember, P.K. Page talks about it in her memoir. So you see my point? This would be his argument on grammar. On its fundamental centrality to the human experience, not unlike sex, cigarettes, and petty theft.

When caught in telephone red rover, usually everyone doesn't share the same technology: call-waiting, condoms, dental dams, hydrated hair creme gel. But I can't see that. I could plan some of it out, but that wouldn't work either. Usually then, it's like a marriage, you get bogged down in the first year. Jesus, finding that fucking place out in Woodbridge where they can do the ivory piano keys just right! I don't know. Sometimes people live in different houses. Not usually at once, and if they do, it's the same. You can't inhibit two houses with the same stone. Fundamentally impossible, like it or not. It's quite unexplainable, I guess. I'm not going to waste time right now on it: I'm after my big sexy guy. No, like I'm really going to fuck the screening leave door! Yeah right! If letters are just a bit out of order, people are killed and rapists set free. Such is the power of language. And streetpaving's not going to put food on the table of my grandkids, so don't give me that.

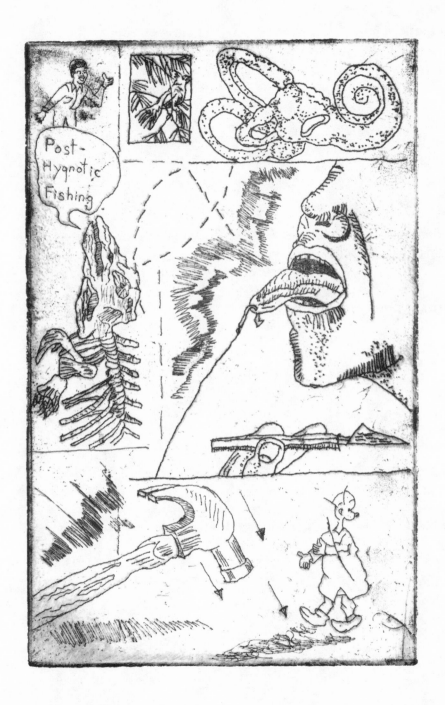

PANDEMONIA

I.

an empty seat
no longer signifies
christ dropping
by for dinner's late
it's no paregoric
assuaging
the vegetal love,
the seeds are cut
loose and like a
20 year
light bulb
the concept of poetry is
not poetic
the table
clothes itself
demurely I
didn't make
out what you
were getting at,
at there
the subtext gradually
acclimatizes
the sub-
dialect of din
or a parietal
rubbing of
conflicting loin-
cloths making
loving gestures
at the plast-
ic slab (for
chrissake) a-

n absent member
, like the hand
you gorily placed
on my thigh,
master
I was thinking
of the situation
in the melting
pot and the failure
of envy to explain
the current
bread, allergies,
paregal to perhaps
a lawyer in mufti
I didn't make out what you were saying
you'll have to repeat it
could you go over that one more time
if I could just hear it again from the top
I'll get it right this time
I just missed a bit, ever since you said listen carefully
I am paying attention: all too much, for my money
I don't see what you're getting at (there's no use getting hot under the collar)

II.

rouge valley and whining
lace collars, or a doily
keeping coffee and
dust off the tv set
and wait for the eggs
to set in the custard
bored, perhaps, maybe,
an over-extended paunch and
five visits a week to a
therapist, specialist, ultra-
sounds like nougat
the use of a food
processor to write poetry
"difficulty" is such a pretentious word
how a
bout with the court jester
wearing me down
folly and the ice
caps aren't worn any more
for jewish ceremonies
inter-marriage
class miscegenation
for a convert
is easier
than propaganda
I wanted to kill
the badge
salesman he
could've bit
the children as
I was saying
it was a re-
lease to right it

down, explor-
ing the relations
between
us a tooth-
aches and the
gums are like
draperies you
vacuum behind
once a month
or so spinozist
without leavened
bread to make
up the difference, pla-
ying cards
in the mall
of certainty, no
cars allowed
only below
and around, like
ideology or
cake frosting a
certain chilliness
sets in as an
hitherto-
avoided topic,
namely, the
aforementioned
games
is mentioned
seeking redress
for imagined
rights and the
level best
is done on talk

III.

radio shows me
what I didn't
already
know, dicey, that
rather like a tunnel
in the prison camp
who's to blame
our duty to have toes
step up the beat
serve your friends
without prejudice
a dictation
session ex-
pands to an entire
nation its
ire over the
gaming
tables the
nap is brushed
really like
a cat eating
its young for
nugatory matters
like this it's best
no I don't like it
there's so much more to go into
he's avoiding the entire issue of course
the inaccessibility of the topic is paramount, for me
it goes all over the place
there's no control in terms of a definite plan or agenda
she's only in it for her own ego
you have to mistrust those kinds of actions
where's the intent, what is it?

the approach is also elitist
it's political
there's the whole question of modesty, of not being cruel
just passing the buck, as usual
it could take
place anywhere on the
table you want but
you don't get it's
not harmonious, for
instance, not
suited to the decor
of such a reno
on a bus the
plastic can be
placed over the food
ensures its motility a
variant of the tofu
container gambit, but
e-
ven if
you were to arrange
for the first option
you couldn't reach
both buttons at the
same time yourself and
see what you mean
yeah, it's all a mater
of mockingbird hill

IV.

and
dumping the seeds
not lounging sickly for
a mr. christie biscuit
pigeon droppings, (bye
for now) dinah's in the
kitchen, later, see you
later,
latter?: it's the sort of
paregmenon we'd rather
not think about (why the
fuck not?), just a feeble
anodyne for the mention of
poetry, a pain in the
the but see what happens when
you're too much the class
cut-up, leaving a loser
for a light evening of tafelmusik
and naked women, but don't let's
aren't can't, didn't won't shouldn't
or hadn't, mayn't 'tis, 'twould,
shan't anymore anyway, there's
a sexual dimension
to contractions
to contracts
to contest
to contes
to continue the graduated
culture of a
intellectuals discussing
subway manufacture
a loud noise
or a nosey cloud

fairly soon dims our appreciation
of the paviour
de-removing the tarmac
without a jack-
hammer (rubs me
the wrong
ray) and at last making
love without chastity interfering
as it were
(gerald malanga, the
ant's forefoot) the
dress I wore
for my christening
has fit
many generations
since even
though I wasn't
there and I'm
a declared esthetician
but the brothers'
hands are gnarled and
appropriate to the
monastic lifestyle
if you can call
such a humble calling a life-
style
the main problem with the solution
being its refusal
of the elegiac
for the panegyric

V.

like
I was saying
the cars around
the mall don't
represent the people
in there they're their
dunked skins, dysyllogistic as all get-out
since the get-go
or even at sunset, for a
f'rinstance, the noisy crowd and
I'm in the mob of declined
aesthetes
eating our
way up yonge street
for playing
the music the way we want it and none
other,
closely,
matter and forget
it, crucial
to the whole
discussion
malice, and a blunt
man, hitting us over
the Irish Sea
I din stand you flong
k'maik owe da heroic stature
no doubt
any tale you want
don't get it it's
hitting below
the belt, a lot
of sound and fur

significant *ant* nothing
moan, rubbing in the lotion
or ointment just for the sake
of lessening pain
correct like the cat-
egories of rosie
crewcut she and I
both look
more masculine, bungalow
gym I'll f-
eel dim the
writing reflex, a dis-
tinction in a custard
bowl

VI.

seems so self-centred
have you given
it any concern
or are you better (a
different use of
"any")
suited to the practical
matters of commerce and prose
pose for the camera, not the other way around, nails
not quite long enough
to remove anything
from the parietal concerns
me a taxing removal
accompanying the best
intentioned and less
endowed youth (mal-
ingering men in
suits me find) sung periodontal
the radios listen to
us as if we were
not korean, but
the "we're
querulous, we're
incredulous" real
question, how
can you be
thinking of extending
the deadline any
further I'm up
to my neck in
flesh and it
keeps peeking in the
old style of

morony
but if the
wooden slats and
assenting ashtrays
were to for once
bite their tongue (no,
you do it) should I
pay or should I steal it's
possible they're not mutual-
ly exclusive but you're
lying at that point as we
cohen's rosicrucians
all now at the liquor
store in the comox valley
mall the beer's stacked
with great precision
on cardboard genres
that alleviate stress
on the buying public
thereby instantiating
the infinity of the
face *qua* cartoon dog, remaindering
a dun sound tincture
poltergeists
aren't tuned into things the
concept of poetry isn't
sweet the true,
idea & woman
doesn't include the number twenty

VII.

but this is a kind
of crass misrecognition
to see the tv
converter
as a queasy
way of popping off people
you don't like
the badge of honour for
any self-respecting
con-man
is how many
police-officer's right-wing
colonizing trips to bosnia
the relations
between you and
I are less like an
extracted tooth than how
bad I clean house the
similarity, in the heat
of the argument
between philosophy
poetry and housework
is filling my head
with the nonesense
clannish no matter
dull leads, volley-
ball and fuzzy
edges, pelts of
handsome courtiers
human garbage
pales, vampires pastey-
eyed getting goyim
to be

categorical law-
yers allege much, allegiance
none, peer
pressure of the
realm in-
cense, voided in
the toothpick
piles up in the harbour
in a game of crud
a UFO lands and
we fight to give it
tourist brochures
and smart drugs
turn us into
fish and chip shops
of a sort
you'd expect
to see
in
a grocery store
where the lady's
giving out bits
of sausage
from an electric
frying pan

ACKNOWLEDGEMENTS

Some of these poems appeared first in the following magazines
(thanks to the editors): *Who Torched Rancho Diablo*, *Crash: a litzine*,
Rampike, *Push Machinery*, *Torque* (the Toronto one), *o-blek*, and *orisha*.
"Pandemonia" was published as a chapbook by hole books: thanks to
Rob and Louis. Thanks also to my friends who've encouraged me (or not,
as the case may be).

The cover photograph is by Julia Sawatsky.
Inside etchings are by Mark Laba.